W9-ATY-407

Food Field Trips

Let's Explore
Cookies!

Jill Colella

Lerner Publications ◆ Minneapolis

Hello, Friends,

Everybody eats, even from birth. This is why learning about food is important. Making the right choices about what to eat begins with knowing more about food. Food literacy helps us be curious about food and adventurous about what we eat. In short, it helps us discover how delicious the world of food can be.

I love to eat cookies. I think the best ones are homemade. My favorite cookie of all time is a Christmas cookie that my mom made when I was small. Learning to make cookies is easy. What kind would you like to bake?

For more inspiration, ideas, and recipes, visit www.teachkidstocook.com.

Jill

About the Author
Happy cook, reformed picky eater, and longtime classroom teacher Jill Colella founded both *Ingredient* and *Butternut*, award-winning children's magazines that promote food literacy.

Copyright © 2020 by Lerner Publishing Group, Inc.

All rights reserved. International copyright secured. No part of this book may be reproduced, stored in a retrieval system, or transmitted in any form or by any means—electronic, mechanical, photocopying, recording, or otherwise—without the prior written permission of Lerner Publishing Group, Inc., except for the inclusion of brief quotations in an acknowledged review.

Lerner Publications Company
An imprint of Lerner Publishing Group, Inc.
241 First Avenue North
Minneapolis, MN 55401 USA

For reading levels and more information, look up this title at www.lernerbooks.com.

Main body text set in Mikado. Typeface provided by HVD.

Library of Congress Cataloging-in-Publication Data

Names: Colella, Jill, author.
Title: Let's explore cookies / by Jill Colella.
Description: Minneapolis, MN : Lerner Publications, [2020] | Series: Food field trips | Includes bibliographical references and index.
Identifiers: LCCN 2019011666 (print) | LCCN 2019013924 (ebook) | ISBN 9781541582965 (eb pdf) | ISBN 9781541563018 (lb : alk. paper)
Subjects: LCSH: Cookies—Juvenile literature. | LCGFT: Cookbooks.
Classification: LCC TX772 (ebook) | LCC TX772 .C3868 2020 (print) | DDC 641.86/54—dc23

LC record available at https://lccn.loc.gov/2019011666

Manufactured in the United States of America
1-46463-47540-6/27/2019

SCAN FOR BONUS CONTENT!

Table of Contents

Picture Glossary

bowl

cookie

dough

flour

mix

ALL ABOUT COOKIES

Cookies can be crisp or soft. They can be tiny or large. Cookies can be plain, or they can be full of flavor!

Food gives our bodies energy to move, read, and play. Some foods give our bodies more energy than other foods do.

Why don't we eat only cookies? Cookies taste good, but they do not give us the energy we need. Cookies are good for once in a while.

LET'S COMPARE

Bakers make many different kinds of cookies. Biscotti are crunchy. Gingerbread cookies are spicy! Sugar cookies are cut into shapes.

Snickerdoodles are covered with cinnamon.

Oatmeal cookies are chewy.

Fortune cookies have a message inside. What kind of cookie do you like best?

LET'S EXPLORE

Cookies are made from ingredients like flour, eggs, and butter. These ingredients come from farms.

Wheat grows in fields.
It is milled into flour.

Farmers gather eggs
that hens lay.

Butter is made from milk.
It comes from cows.

LET'S BAKE COOKIES

First, set aside the ingredients. Gather baking powder, eggs, flour, salt, butter, sugar, vanilla, and chocolate chips. These will become cookie dough.

Mix the ingredients in a bowl.
The dough becomes too
stiff to stir with a spoon.

Use your hands
to keep mixing.

What do you
think holds
dough together?

After the dough is mixed, roll it into balls.
Pat the balls into round cookies.

Next, line a pan with parchment paper. Use your hands to place the cookies on a cookie sheet.

When else should you wash your hands?

Sometimes baking gets messy! Wash your hands when you are done.

Count your cookies. How many are there?
A group of twelve is a dozen.

Your cookies are ready to bake! Have an adult help you put them into the oven.

Set a timer so you know when your cookies are done. Peek at them from outside of the oven as they bake.

How do the cookies change as they bake?

When the cookies are golden brown, they are ready to come out of the oven. Be sure to let them cool before you take a bite!

LET'S COOK

What could be easier than making cookies in a microwave? Be careful and use an oven mitt. This recipe makes about 36 cookies. Always remember to have an adult present when working in the kitchen!

NO-BAKE SUPER-EASY COOKIES

INGREDIENTS

- ½ cup (120 ml) milk
- 2 cups (402 g) white sugar
- ½ cup (64 g) cocoa powder
- 1 stick (114 g) butter, cut in chunks
- 3 cups (255 g) quick-cooking oats
- 1 cup (250 g) peanut butter

1. In a microwave-safe bowl, mix the milk, sugar, cocoa, and butter.

2. Microwave on high for 3 minutes. Your mixture should be boiling. If not, microwave for 30 more seconds.

3. Remove the bowl from the microwave.

4. Stir and then return the mixture to the microwave for 3 more minutes, stirring after each minute.

5. Add the oats and peanut butter and stir.

6. Microwave for 1 more minute and stir. Drop spoonfuls of mix onto the wax paper.

7. Place the cookies in the refrigerator to set up.

8. Eat and enjoy!

SEE THIS RECIPE IN ACTION!

LET'S MAKE

COOKIE GIFT JARS

You can layer some basic ingredients in a jar to create a double chocolate cookie mix that you can gift. Practice measuring as you fill the jar.

INGREDIENTS

- ½ cup (110 g) brown sugar
- ½ cup (100 g) white sugar
- ½ cup (64 g) cocoa powder
- ½ teaspoon baking soda
- 1 teaspoon baking powder
- 1 cup (140 g) flour
- 1 cup (175 g) chocolate chips
- ¼ cup (45 g) white chocolate chips

1. Carefully scoop the above ingredients into a glass jar to create layers. (Hint: Gently tap the jar on a table or countertop to make pretty, even layers.)

2. Copy the ingredients list and steps on the next page onto an index card, and attach it to the mix.

DOUBLE CHOCOLATE COOKIES

INGREDIENTS

- 1 jar cookie mix
- 6 tablespoons (85 g) butter, softened
- 2 eggs, beaten
- parchment paper–lined baking sheets (or well-greased baking sheets)

1. An adult should preheat the oven to 350°F (180°C).
2. Empty the jar into a large mixing bowl and stir.
3. In a separate bowl, use an electric mixer to cream together butter and eggs. They should be light and fluffy.
4. Add about half the dry ingredients to the eggs and butter.
5. Use the mixer to mix the dry ingredients.
6. Spoon in the remaining dry ingredients bit by bit and keep mixing.
7. Use a spoon to drop tablespoons of dough 2 inches (5 cm) apart on baking sheets.
8. Bake for 13 to 15 minutes. If not firm, bake 2 to 3 more minutes.

Let's Read

Hoffmann, Sara E. *Nia Bakes Cookies*. Minneapolis: LernerClassroom, 2014.

Home Baking
http://www.homebaking.org

Kuskowski, Alex. *Super Simple Classic Cookies: Easy Cookie Recipes for Kids!* Minneapolis: Abdo, 2015.

Nieminen, Lotta. *Cookies! An Interactive Recipe Book*. New York: Phaidon, 2018.

Ransom, Candice. *Chocolate Chip Cookies*. Minneapolis: Pop, 2019 .

Texas Wheat
http://texaswheat.org

Index

Photo Acknowledgments

Image credits: Pixel-Shot/Shutterstock.com, p. 1; Nick Lundgren/Shutterstock.com, p. 3 (dough); VictorH11/Shutterstock.com, p. 3 (bowl); M. Unal Ozmen/Shutterstock.com, p. 3 (flour); tanatat/Shutterstock.com, p. 3 (cookie); Wavebreakmedia/iStock/Getty Images, p. 3 (mix); YAKOBCHUK VIACHESLAV/Shutterstock.com, p. 4; LauriPatterson/E+/Getty Images, p. 5 (top); Ariel Skelley/DigitalVision/Getty Images, pp. 5 (bottom left), 13; iuliia_n/Shutterstock.com, p. 5 (bottom right); Ekaterina Smirnova/Shutterstock.com, p. 6 (top); Jose Luis Pelaez Inc/DigitalVision/Getty Images, p. 6 (bottom left); pixelheadphoto digitalskillet/Shutterstock.com, p. 6 (bottom right); Mny-Jhee/Shutterstock.com, p. 7 (top); MikeMartin/Shutterstock.com, p. 7 (middle right); Teri Virbickis/Shutterstock.com, p. 7 (bottom); Marie C Fields/Shutterstock.com, p. 8 (snickerdoodle); MSPhotographic/Shutterstock.com, p. 8 (oatmeal cookie); pick-uppath/iStock/Getty Images, p. 8 (fortune cookie); Ron and Patty Thomas/E+/Getty Images, p. 9; 5 second Studio/Shutterstock.com, p. 10 (top); PhotoSongserm/Shutterstock.com, p. 10 (bottom left); Alexander Chaikin/Shutterstock.com, p. 10 (bottom right); Arina P Habich/Shutterstock.com, p. 11; Mike Kemp/Getty Images, p. 12 (top); Tracy Garbett/Shutterstock.com, p. 12 (middle left); Ryan Cutler/EyeEm/Getty Images, p. 14; Evgeny Atamanenko/Shutterstock.com, p. 15 (top); Bignai/Shutterstock.com, p. 15 (bottom); VDB Photos/Shutterstock.com, p. 16; Brand X Pictures/Stockbyte/Getty Images, p. 17; Natasha Sioss/Moment/Getty Images, p. 18 (top); JohnnyH5/iStock/Getty Images, p. 18 (bottom); Thomas M Perkins/Shutterstock.com, p. 19; P Maxwell Photography/Shutterstock.com, p. 20 (top); Laura Westlund/Independent Picture Service, pp. 20, 21, 22 (illustrations); Malinkaphoto/iStock/Getty Images, p. 22 (top).

Front cover: Pinkyone/Shutterstock.com (ingredients); tmcphotos/Shutterstock.com (girl); melissamn/Shutterstock.com (cookies); eggeegg/Shutterstock.com (children). Back cover: Anna Kurzaeva/Moment/Getty Images.